Ferlinghetti
Portrait

First Edition

01 00 99 98   4 3 2 1

Published by
Gibbs Smith, Publisher
P.O. Box 667
Layton, UT 84041
Orders: (1-800) 748-5439
Visit our web site at www.gibbs-smith.com

Editor: Gail Yngve
Designer: Brad Thomas
Photo Editor: Marilla Pearsall
Copy Editors: Joyce Jenkins, Richard Silberg, Marilla Pearsall
Acknowledgment: Rita Bottoms, Bill McPheron, Tony Bliss
Master Prints: Kirk Anspach
Consultant: John Yau

Printed in Asia

Library of Congress Cataloging-in-Publication Data

Ferlinghetti, Lawrence.
Ferlinghetti portrait / poetry by Lawrence Ferlinghetti;
photography by Christopher Felver.
p.   cm.
ISBN 0-87905-851-X
1. Beat generation—Poetry. 2. Ferlinghetti, Lawrence—Portraits.
3. Poets, American—20th century—Portraits. 4. Beat generation—
Pictorial works. I. Felver, Christopher, 1946– . II. Title.
PS3511.E557A6 1998
811'.54—dc21   98-18051
CIP

GIBBS·SMITH

PUBLISHER

SALT LAKE CITY

Ferlinghetti
Portrait

CHRISTOPHER FELVER

The Gods and the Tramp

"The young poet is a god. The old poet is a tramp."
—Wallace Stevens

In one photograph, we are looking at the good grey Allen Ginsberg staring warily at paintings, and the poet-painter Lawrence Ferlinghetti bent over and looking closer, a black tie dangling like a clause. Allen is standing in front of a famous portrait of himself by Elaine de Kooning that she rendered quickly on television. We are entranced and boxed into this happy corner. The paintings matter, but looking matters more to gods and tramps who love to look at anything, nothing. Allen leans on his umbrella like a "pliant cane," and both are truly grey (Rimbaud: *chenu de chagrin*, or gone grey with pain). The whole is as musical and melancholy as transactions in contemplation in Daumier's "artist" series. Here the world of celebrity is calmed down into a quiet pocket of celebration.

The anarchist theme and heritage spreads out here and derives in part from Rexroth as much as from Bakunin. One sees this libertarian politics in LF's Statue of Liberty paintings, with their bleeding if not Situationist graffiti. That a street should be named after Ferlinghetti, and that Felver captured this hopeful event is not, as they say, coincidental. It would be as appropriate as having a Pollock square in Manhattan—but it does not exist. That Ferlinghetti has had this coronation—like Ginsberg in Prague—is a sign of his extreme and fruitful work. The nude in his drawings and paintings conjures up the best nudity of his freely enjambed poems. His famous "Goya" poem shows, however, the seriousness of his sense of terror in the empire of pure products: "strange license plates / and engines that devour America." Like the anarchist Barnett Newman, Ferlinghetti's career in any media is always political in the radical sense of the urban spaces with which it collaborates. The poet revitalizes the theory of camaraderie as dissent.

Felver has developed a taste for this dissident happiness. Koch's subversive insight about St-John Perse remains—that we need to have the courage to stare into beauty as much as into the abyss. The generosity of this Lucretian skepticism emerges like a contagious paradox. LF has created our central marginal bookstore of independence, and the only analogies East are the Gotham Book Mart, with its saint of poetry, Miss Steloff, and the Grolier in Boston still activated by Louise Solano. Visitors from Germany have told me they were searching for these stores because nothing is like them elsewhere. The bookstore functions like a government of one. Beyond this, of course, we are looking at the face of one who created the dazzlingly fresh list of City Lights within his own Chaplinesque taste. *Lunch Poems, Howl, Kaddish*—these and a hundred more (Corso, Lamantia, Patchen, Serge) signify the gigantic notion of the American anarchist: generosity and potlatch as transgression. At the Old West Hotel, with the intrepid anarchist phrase dangling from our own eighteenth-century enlightened radicalism (Don't Tread On Me) the poet, happy as a cowboy Whitman, welcomes all in front of his shack like a saloon. The picture reminds me also that the landscape matches this human mood in a drastic diagonal above, and the finesse of trees and leaves is not deleted in the upper left. "Don't Tread on Me" underlines the essential topos that the saint Meyer Shapiro—a teacher of Allen Ginsberg—found in Abstract Expressionism: defiance on behalf of a humane liberty. If we learn anything from the poet's Whitmanesque slouch and the happiness in all his poetry and paintings, it is this superb note. And just as the aging art historian noted that his greatest regret was the defeat of socialism in his time, so one feels throughout all these photos a superb melancholy about a country destroying its air and land without contrition.

Felver is not only an eye, but an eye connected to an odd and compellingly hopeful mind. I connect this principle of hope with the face seen everywhere here—a sign of clarity and resolve. The group of listeners at a reading is as important as the enshrined poet. Reception is all and why I have grown to admire Felver's instantaneities is his willingness to break the psychological taboo.

There are those who enjoy the Beat phenomenon as an adolescent sociology or a Utopian failure, and there are those who are still indeed at war with Allen Ginsberg. We must say there is an appropriate sense in which reactionaries still have a problem with Allen and LF. What makes the Right still restless with this group is the taste that can never be completely transcended of an anti-imperial dissent and a pacifist momentum. There is in Felver not just a nostalgic taste for bohemia, but an openness to the Daumier-like satire that is within these temporary shelters and aging gods. I recall that Arthur A. Cohen, then vice-president of Holt, Rinehart, and Winston, was bemused and respectful of Allen Ginsberg's choice not to leave LF for a large publisher. Cohen understood immediately what this noble gesture meant in democratic space. Ferlinghetti and the alarming Burroughs; F and the ecstatic Cage; F in his bookstore like a kingdom—these are images of the anarcho-syndicalist. It is easy for the reactionary Right to maintain their resentments and speak of the slovenly poetics or the real-world consequence of addiction. What it cannot abide is the continuing tradition of dissent that argues that America is not to be a universal policeman or army state.

The best photography must have the Negative Capability to look at everyone and everything without contempt. The shameless fullness of Felver's art follows this drastic rule. When I was young I ran away in a much-rehearsed desire to sense the space of America and bottle a bit of the Pacific Ocean. In the poet LF, Felver has rediscovered the space and the bottle. And though some think the genie should stay in the bottle, these are artists who are unafraid to let the genie out, wild.

David Shapiro
Riverdale, NYC, April 5, 1998

While traveling west for the summer in 1966, I discovered City Lights Bookstore. There in the midst of the Broadway scene of strip-joints, bars, and sailor hangouts was the West Coast vortex of rebel literary life. I watched from the sidelines as poetry was spontaneously read, jazz wailed, the Fillmore bands played to full houses, and the fervent idealism of the '60s crested. I left San Francisco and returned to Coconut Grove and college, but California stayed with me. I didn't return for ten years, during which time I got thrown out of the army and found salvation after at Alice's Restaurant and David Silverstein's bookstore in the Berkshires. I immersed myself in reading; Neal Cassady's, *The First Third* and Ginsberg's photographs in Ann Charter's *Scenes Off The Road*, both City Lights Books, were two visions with which I strongly identified. I moved about North America, guitar in hand, with the same sense of poetic wandering and vagabond discovery that this gang of bards seemed to be celebrating.

I returned to San Francisco in '76 intending to get involved in the scene. A May Day reading at the Spaghetti Factory on Grant Street featured local poets including Ferlinghetti. The reading was electrifying—so many impassioned voices! I decided right then and there to document what I saw happening.

Gregory Corso lived in North Beach as did Bob Kaufman, Philip Lamantia, Neeli Cherkovski, Jack Hirschman, and Howard Hart. Philip Whalen lived across town at the Zen Center and McClure in the Haight. Ginsberg kept passing through on the way to some-where, anywhere. Burroughs was in the wings, Snyder in the Sierra. There were daily venues for poetic action: the Intersection for the Arts, Savoy Tivoli, the Kabuki Theater, and especially City Lights.

One day I stopped at Lawrence's Francisco Street flat to do a portrait; we started talking. Let's just say we had the same esthetic, a leaning toward paint and literature. I thought it might be a good idea to make an experimental video of a poem, but it was somehow decided that I film his paintings at the Fort Mason Armory Show. That first shoot became the inadvertent beginning of a fifteen-year documentary, *The Coney Island of Lawrence Ferlinghetti.*

Ferlinghetti has a tremendous sense of humor. For the longest time I wanted him to give me a straight answer. No dice. He comments in a funny way on most everything he sees, and he's as sharp as an eagle. Situations just stack up interestingly to him. He is forever the optimist.

When Ferlinghetti travels, he looks like a country doctor on call: one small leather bag with a change of clothes, just the essentials. In reporter notebooks he constantly writes observations and poems. He reads voraciously, particularly local newspapers. Lawrence is fluent in whatever Romance language is spoken. He's comfortable getting about in the world.

We traveled to Nicaragua together in '84. Ernesto Cardenal had invited Lawrence to the Rubén Darío poetry festival. Ferlinghetti had just published *Volcan*, an anthology of Central American poetry, and we arrived in Managua with a fresh case of books. We were quartered in Somocista housing, locked into our rooms with an armed guard. Ferlinghetti was the avid reporter, detached, not taking sides, balancing all that came at him. During his reading before the *compañeros*, Lawrence presented Ernesto with a seed from Pasternak's grave. For Nicaraguans to have Ferlinghetti in their country symbolized solidarity. My photographs and our notes became the book *Seven Days in Nicaragua Libre*.

Thirteen miles south of Monterey is Lawrence's Bixby Canyon cabin, the world's smallest Victorian: ten by twelve feet with bed, camping gear, sharpened ax, and stone-manteled fireplace. Outside is a stream, a windmill atop a water drum, the outhouse. The sun sets early up the canyon and dinner is cooked outside over a campfire. Kerouac wrote *Big Sur* here, and Beat myths are endless. I've always treasured time here, especially spinning tall tales into the evening fires. The nights are cold in coastal California; I pull my sleeping bag tight around me in The Temple of the Zen Fool and dream of days of yore.

Allen Ginsberg was Lawrence's lifelong friend. When Allen was in town, there was most assuredly an event scheduled at City Lights. Every year Lawrence nominated Allen for the Nobel Prize. We were in New York a week after Allen died and went over to Ginsberg's new loft on 13th Street. Peter Orlovsky was watering the flowers as a vigil while Bill Morgan, Lawrence, and I chatted in the bedroom overlooking 1st Avenue. For Lawrence it was the twilight of a heartfelt relationship that lasted over forty years. At the end of the conversation I bowed out so Lawrence could take a snooze in Allen's guest room. Allen's presence or the lack of was hard on all, and it seemed everyone was lingering a little longer among Allen's artifacts that were so perfectly arranged in his new digs.

Lawrence lives two blocks walking distance from City Lights Books. The bookstore is in "little old wooden North Beach," the city's answer to Little Italy, loaded with coffee shops and a general feeling of bohemia. When Lawrence put his shingle out, poets promptly gathered to read, hang out, or just talk. It is like a salon that hosts book parties, poetry readings, and events where like-minded and opinionated acquaintances gather. The alley adjacent to City Lights has since been renamed Kerouac Alley, and across the street is Saroyan Alley next to Spec's Bar and Cafe Tosca. Many streets have been renamed after writers who haunted the city. Ferlinghetti spearheaded the street renaming project. In short, Lawrence is as much a part of San Francisco as the famous hills and fog.

These photographs came naturally, on the spur of the moment while on the road or just hanging out. We usually laughed while snapping them, not taking anything too seriously. One rainy day we walked by Via Ferlinghetti, the alley that was once the site of bootleggers and undertakers. We stopped and laughed as Lawrence reminded me, "It's the perfect place for poets to hang out."

Beneath his bowler, Ferlinghetti's eyes radiate the Chaplinesque spirit that fuels his indomitable zest and compassion for others. In all the adventures we've shared together "lo these many years," I always feel at home in his presence. Lawrence has become a dear friend.

Christopher Felver

FELVER pursued me
over the hills + dales of
painting + poetry,
catching the highlights +
lowlights of a lifetime
fomenting art + anarchy

Ferlinghetti
3/98
"Death to the State"

Francisco Street '97

AUTOBIOGRAPHY

I am leading a quiet life
in Mike's Place every day
watching the champs
of the Dante Billiard Parlor
and the French pinball addicts.
I am leading a quiet life
on lower East Broadway.
I am an American.
I was an American boy.
I read the American Boy Magazine
and became a boy scout
in the suburbs.
I thought I was Tom Sawyer
catching crayfish in the Bronx River
and imagining the Mississippi.
I had a baseball mitt
and an American Flyer bike.
I delivered the Woman's Home Companion
at five in the afternoon
or the Herald Trib
at five in the morning.
I still can hear the paper thump
on lost porches.
I had an unhappy childhood.
I saw Lindberg land.
I looked homeward
and saw no angel.
I got caught stealing pencils
from the Five and Ten Cent Store
the same month I made Eagle Scout.
I chopped trees for the CCC

Provincetown '94

and sat on them.
I landed in Normandy
in a rowboat that turned over.
I have seen the educated armies
on the beach at Dover.
I have seen Egyptian pilots in purple clouds'
shopkeepers rolling up their blinds
at midday
potato salad and dandelions
at anarchist picnics.
I am reading 'Lorna Doone'
and a life of John Most
terror of the industrialist
a bomb on his desk at all times.
I have seen the garbagemen parade
in the Columbus Day Parade
behind the glib
farting trumpeters.
I have not been out to the Cloisters
in a long time
nor to the Tuileries
but I still keep thinking
of going.
I have seen the garbagemen parade
when it was snowing.
I have eaten hotdogs in ballparks.
I have heard the Gettysburg Address
and the Ginsberg Address.
I like it here
and I won't go back
where I came from.

City Lights '80

I too have ridden boxcars boxcars boxcars.
I have travelled among unknown men.
I have been in Asia
with Noah in the Ark.
I was in India
when Rome was built.
I have been in the Manger
with an Ass.
I have seen the Eternal Distributor
from a White Hill
in South San Francisco
and the Laughing Woman at Loona Park
outside the Fun House
in a great rainstorm
still laughing.
I have heard the sound of revelry
by night.
I have wandered lonely
as a crowd.
I am leading a quiet life
outside of Mike's Place every day
watching the world walk by
in its curious shoes.
I once started out
to walk around the world
but ended up in Brooklyn.
That Bridge was too much for me.
I have engaged in silence
exile and cunning.
I flew too near the sun
and my wax wings fell off.

Hunters Point '93

I am looking for my Old Man
whom I never knew.
I am looking for the Lost Leader
with whom I flew.
Young men should be explorers.
Home is where one starts from.
But Mother never told me
there'd be scenes like this.
Womb-weary
I rest
I have travelled.
I have seen goof city.
I have seen the mass mess.
I have heard Kid Ory cry.
I have heard a trombone preach.
I have heard Debussy
strained thru a sheet.
I have slept in a hundred islands
where books were trees.
I have heard the birds
that sound like bells.
I have worn grey flannel trousers
and walked upon the beach of hell.
I have dwelt in a hundred cities
where trees were books.
What subways what taxis what cafes!
What women with blind breasts
limbs lost among skyscrapers!
I have seen the statues of heroes
at carrefours.
Danton weeping at a metro entrance

Ellis Island '94

Columbus in Barcelona
pointing Westward up the Ramblas
toward the American Express
Lincoln in his stony chair
And a great Stone Face
in North Dakota.
I know that Columbus
did not invent America.
I have heard a hundred housebroken Ezra Pounds.
They should all be freed.
It is long since I was a herdsman.
I am leading a quiet life
in Mike's Place every day
reading the Classified columns.
I have read the Reader's Digest
from cover to cover
and noted the close identification
of the United States and the Promised Land
where every coin is marked
In God We Trust
but the dollar bills do not have it
being gods unto themselves.
I read the Want Ads daily
looking for a stone a leaf
an unfound door.
I hear America singing
in the Yellow Pages.
One could never tell
the soul has its rages.
I read the papers every day
and hear humanity amiss

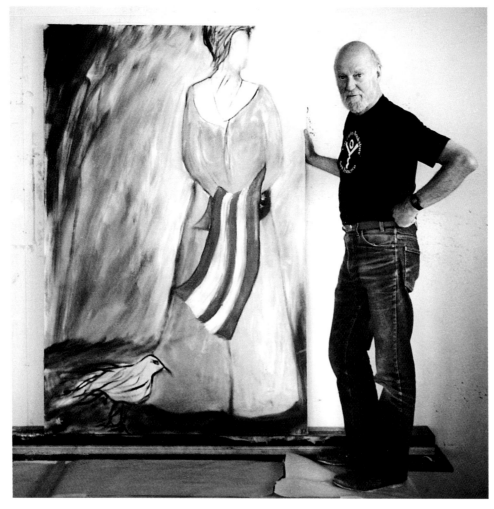

Hunters Point '88

in the sad plethora of print.
I see where Walden Pond has been drained
to make an amusement park.
I see they're making Melville
eat his whale.
I see another war is coming
but I won't be there to fight it.
I have read the writing
on the outhouse wall.
I helped Kilroy write it.
I marched up Fifth Avenue
blowing on a bugle in a tight platoon
but hurried back to the Casbah
looking for my dog.
I see a similarity
between dogs and me.
Dogs are the true observers
walking up and down the world
thru the Moloy country.
I have walked down alleys
too narrow for Chryslers.
I have seen a hundred horseless milkwagons
in a vacant lot in Astoria.
Ben Shahn never painted them
but they're there
askew in Astoria.
I have heard the junkman's obbligato.
I have ridden superhighways
and believed the billboard's promises
Crossed the Jersey Flats
and seen the Cities of the Plain

Francisco Street '82

and wallowed in the wilds of Westchester
with its roving bands of natives
in stationwagons.
I have seen them.
I am the man.
I was there.
I suffered
somewhat.
I am an American.
I have a passport.
I did not suffer in public.
And I'm too young to die.
I am a selfmade man.
And I have plans for the future.
I am in line
for a top job.
I may be moving on
to Detroit.
I am only temporarily
a tie salesman.
I am a good Joe.
I am an open book
to my boss.
I am a complete mystery
to my closest friends.
I am leading a quiet life
in Mike's Place every day
contemplating my navel.
I am part
of the body's long madness.
I have wandered in various nightwoods.

Hunters Point '98

I have leaned in drunken doorways.
I have written wild stories
without punctuation.
I am the man.
I was there.
I suffered
somewhat.
I have sat in an uneasy chair.
I am a tear of the sun.
I am a hill
where poets run.
I invented the alphabet
after watching the flight of cranes
who made letters with their legs.
I am a lake upon a plain.
I am a word
in a tree.
I am a hill of poetry.
I am a raid
on the inarticulate.
I have dreamt
that all my teeth fell out
but my tongue lived
to tell the tale.
For I am a still
of poetry.
I am a bank of song.
I am a playerpiano
in an abandoned casino
on a seaside esplanade
in a dense fog

Hunters Point '86

still playing.
I see a similarity
between the Laughing Woman
and myself.
I have heard the sound of summer
in the rain.
I have seen girls on boardwalks
have complicated sensations.
I understand their hesitations.
I am a gatherer of fruit.
I have seen how kisses
cause euphoria.
I have risked enchantment.
I have seen the Virgin
in an appletree at Chartres
And Saint Joan burn
at the Bella Union.
I have seen giraffes in junglejims
their necks like love
wound around the iron circumstances
of the world.
I have seen the Venus Aphrodite
armless in her drafty corridor.
I have heard a siren sing
at One Fifth Avenue.
I have seen the White Goddess dancing
in the Rue des Beaux Arts
on the Fourteenth of July
and the Beautiful Dame Without Mercy
picking her nose in Chumley's.
She did not speak English.

North Beach '96

She had yellow hair
and a hoarse voice
and no bird sang.
I am leading a quiet life
in Mike's Place every day
watching the pocket pool players
making the minestrone scene
wolfing the macaronis
and I have read somewhere
the Meaning of Existence
yet have forgotten
just exactly where.
But I am the man
And I'll be there.
And I may cause the lips
of those who are asleep
to speak.
And I may make my notebooks
into sheaves of grass
And I may write my own
eponymous epitaph
instructing the horsemen
to pass.

City Lights '81

Allen Ginsberg, LF,
Nancy Peters '81

LF, Nancy Peters, John Cage '86

William Burroughs, LF '81

City Lights '95

David Gascoyne, LF '81

City Lights '83

City Lights '81

Kerouac Alley '95

City Lights '95

Hunters Point '95

DeYoung Museum '96

Armory Show '82

Francisco Street '82

Hunters Point '86

Hunters Point '86

Gregory Corso, LF '81

North Beach '80

Allen Ginsberg, LF '81

Gary Snyder, LF   Golden Gate University '80

Francisco Street '81

Francisco Street '81

Bixby Canyon '84

Bixby Canyon '94

Bixby Canyon '95

Bixby Canyon '95

Bixby Canyon '97

Bixby Canyon '97

Bixby Canyon '95

Bixby Beach '95

Solentname, Nicaragua '84

Peñas Blancas, Nicaragua '84

Managua '84

Managua '84

Juan Bañuelos, Julio Valle,
Father Ernesto Cardenal, Luis Rocha,
Fernando Silva, LF, '84

Managua '84

Battery Park '94

Allen Ginsberg, LF   New York University '94

Allen Ginsberg, LF   New York University '94

Gregory Corso, LF   New York University '94

Andrei Voznesensky, LF   New York University '94

New York '85

Cafe Puccini '80

Francisco Street '98

LF, Allen Ginsberg City Lights '96

Francisco Street '81

LF, Ted Joans '80

Cafe Puccini '80

City Lights '97

City Lights '97

George Whitman, Marilla Pearsall, LF   Shakespeare & Co., Paris '91

R.G. Michel   Paris '91

Hunters Point '88

Hunters Point '98

Francisco Street '97

Bolinas '98

Sausalito '98

San Francisco Bay, '95

Provincetown '94

Gary Snyder, LF,
Michael McClure
Marin County '95

Francisco Street '82

Francisco Street '82

City Lights '95

Washington Square Park '95

Amiri Baraka, LF   Boulder, '94

David T. Dellinger, LF   Boulder, '94

Bixby Canyon '95

Bixby Canyon '84

Bixby Canyon '97

Bixby Canyon '97

Bixby Canyon '97

Bolinas '98

City Lights '98

LF, Julie Ferlinghetti Daytona Beach '84

LF, Jing, Leonardo, Lorenzo Ferlinghetti   Bolinas '98

City Lights '95

Francisco Street '97

Via Ferlinghetti '95

Via Ferlinghetti '95